## *Foreword*

So, you've got a maths exam coming up? Well, that sucks.[1]

This book is a last-minute panic guide to making sure you pick up all of the marks available to you in the exam. It's not here to teach you any new mathematical topics (although I'll mention some in passing); it's not here to help you with a long-term revision plan (although there may be some hints here and there).

It's here to help you get as prepared as you can, as quickly as you can, so that you score as highly as you can.

To do that, there are two broad strategies:
- Pick up extra marks
- Avoid mistakes that cost you marks

You'll also need to have your head on straight, and have a plan for how, in detail, you're going to tackle the exam.

If you think of anything I've missed out or you think I'm leading you astray, you can drop me an email (I'm colin@flyingcoloursmaths.co.uk) or catch me on twitter (@icecolbeveridge). I look forward to hearing from you!

... and best of luck with the exam. Give it your best shot!

# CHAPTER ONE

## *The day before*

The day before the exam is probably as late as you can leave it to learn something new. Unless you're a genius, it's probably beyond you to learn the whole syllabus from scratch in a day; depending on what you know, you should set your goals accordingly:

- If you know practically nothing, you should probably be aiming to get enough marks to pass. That may or may not be realistic, but it's the lowest meaningful barrier you can aim to clear. Find some topics that look simple enough to get on top of and focus on those.

- If you have enough knowledge that you'd expect to pass, I'd suggest looking at the borderline topics — places where you typically get two marks out of four. These are places where you already have a fair foundation to build on, and may be able to turn those two marks into three or four.

- If you're in a good place and expect to do well, what on earth are you doing with this book? Give it to someone who needs it! More seriously, try to figure out what's stopping you from getting 100% — what are the typical mistakes you make? Are there areas where you slip up? See if you can get your head into those.

The day before the exam, I'd recommend splitting your time between *practice* — doing maths; *preparation* — making resources that will help you; and *panic-learning* — cramming anything you still haven't quite got into your head.

The better you feel about things, the more you can focus on the first two things; the lower your confidence, the more you ought to work on the second two.

## *Review topics*

If you haven't already, the day before your exam is a great time to see what you're supposed to know for the exam. To do this, you're going to need a list of topics.

There are several places you may get one of these. Your

teacher may have provided you with one which is now loitering somewhere in a forgotten exercise book. You may get out your textbook and copy the chapter and topic headings. Or you may fire up the Googles and search for (e.g.) "Maths GCSE topics list".

Once you have the topics list, I like to do a "smiley face" survey of them. (Others do a "traffic lights" survey or a "1-5" survey, but they all boil down to the same thing.) For each topic in turn, decide whether you're confident (big smile/green light/5), completely at a loss (big frown/red light/1) or somewhere in between — and draw the appropriate symbol on your list.

With this in place, you can make a last-minute study plan. I find the most helpful order to do last-minute revision is to focus on the neither-happy-nor-sad faces, the topics where you have some knowledge but aren't completely confident. These are places where you have a bit of background knowledge and where your work will have the biggest effect — it's generally earlier to turn a "two out of four" question into 4/4 than it is to turn a "zero out of four" into 2/4.

If you have time after looking at those areas, look at the sad faces and see which ones offer a glimmer of a smile —

can these turn into slightly less miserable outlooks? Can you find ways of picking up the odd mark here and there on these?

Lastly, spend a little time on your happy faces to try to keep them happy — do a few practice questions and make sure you're getting full marks on those.

## *Make a cheat sheet*

If you're watching a movie, and someone (annoyingly) asks you what that relatively minor character's name is, you'll probably be able to answer instantly without thinking about it. If you're on Pointless a few months later and a still of the character pops up, his or her name is unlikely to be on the tip of your tongue.

That's the difference between short-term and long-term memory. When you're involved in something, it's easy to know details about what's just recently happened; once some time has passed, it's much harder — so the stuff you covered in Year 8 isn't necessarily easy to remember, but what you reviewed yesterday might be easier.

See where I'm going with this?

One way to hack your mind into remembering more stuff is to cram it, in the hours before you go into the exam, with details you expect to need to remember. You can do this with a *cheat sheet*. It's not really a cheat (you're not going to take it into the exam, you're just going to remember what's on it), but it's so effective it might as well be! Here's what you do:

- Pick 6 to 10 formulas or facts you're going to need in the exam
- Write these on a bit of paper

Difficult, huh? Well, of course, there's a bit more to it than that. You're going to write them on a bit of paper in such a way that they're easy to remember. Some suggestions:

- Use colour and pictures to highlight various things. It's easier to remember "I wrote that equation in blue and red next to the picture of my favourite singer" than "I put it in the top-left corner".
- If you have an explanation for the things you're writing down, write that down as well — but that's just to help you remember the formula/fact, you don't need to remember the whole explanation!
- Test yourself several times by trying to recreate the

sheet from memory. Check against the original and fix any errors and omissions.

The idea is, you'll look over the cheat sheet just before you go in, and jot down the important facts somewhere convenient on the exam paper once the exam has started.

## *Do a paper*

Once you've got your cheat sheet done, one of the most powerful things you can do the day before your exam is to run through a past paper. Don't worry too much about exam conditions (unless you know you struggle with the time constraints) — concentrate on getting through the material and figuring out where you've got a few weaknesses to fill in.

While it's unlikely that you'll get *exactly* the same question in your real exam as you do in your practice paper, you're likely to see the same *style* of question. This might either jog your memory, or remind you that you needed to check exactly how to answer that kind of question, so that when it comes up tomorrow, ta-da! Marks in the bank.

It also helps you get into the habit of reading

'examinese', the weird language exam questions are written in. It's quite like English, in some respects, but tends to say things like "There are $n$ pens in a bag" instead of using numbers like a normal person would. (It's ok: in examinese, $n$ is a number, and you can do sums with it just like you would, say, seven.)

Taking a couple of hours to work through a past paper the day before helps get forgetful errors out of the way, helps put you in the 'answering maths questions' frame of mind, and helps take some of the fear of the unknown away from the paper.

## *Mark a paper*

Mark your paper? Isn't that somebody else's job?

Well, technically, yes, it's usually someone else's job to mark your work. However, marking your *own* work, carefully and honestly, is one of the best ways to understand how you can improve. When you do maths homework, do you just rattle it off and hand it in, or do you check to make sure it's right? When you get it back, do you go through and say "I got that wrong — how come? What's gone wrong there?"

There are two main advantages to analysing your work like this: firstly, you get an insight into what the examiners want to see — where, exactly, you get the marks in a four-mark question; what kind of language they want to see in an 'explain...' answer. The second advantage is, you give yourself pretty immediate feedback on your work, so you can easily see where you're making errors you can easily fix — and where you can pick up cheap bonus marks for (say) writing down appropriate formulas even if you don't know the topic inside out.

You can (almost certainly) get hold of a mark scheme from the same place that you got the paper you did. There's quite a lot of jargon involved (all the A2, B1 and M0 stuff that's a headache even for me, as well as things like 'oe' (or equivalent) and 'awrt' (anything which rounds to).) These are generally explained somewhere in the first few pages.

Tip: Don't worry too much about totting up your marks, unless you're really curious about your score. It's not a good idea to compare your score in one paper to another one you've done, as some exams are harder than others — if you do want to check your progress, you can look for grade boundaries online and compare the grades you got in each paper (and how far you were from the next grade up).

If you can find an Examiner's Report, that's even more of a goldmine for information about the exam — here, you can read up on what the examiners found frustrating or annoying, the traps that students fell into, and — reading between the lines — things you should look out for when you do your paper.

# CHAPTER TWO

## *Just before*

Only once, in all of the exams I've ever sat, have I ever woken up on exam morning and said "I'm as prepared as I can be; I'm not going to do any more work before the test." I walked to the beach, watched the sun come up, said hello to a friendly dog and an aggressive seagull, and then I aced the exam.

Unusually, I'd got my stress in early, had a good day of extremely hard group revision the day before, gone to bed feeling pretty confident, and planned my morning accordingly. Normally, I'd have taken a much more panicked approach.

Short-term and long-term memory work in much different ways — your long-term memory is full of the stuff you've learned over the whole of your course, but you can fill your short-term memory with useful facts and formulas on the day, and (with any luck) pick up a few marks that you wouldn't otherwise have got.

On that morning, I didn't skip breakfast, though; that would have been madness. And I didn't leave home without running through my checklist of 'things to take to the exam'. Some exam morning rituals are more important to observe than others. In this chapter, I'll take you through some of the last-ditch preparations that have worked for me and for my students.

## *Check equipment*

Before you leave for your exam, you *absolutely must* check that you have everything. Assume the absolute worst about your friends and teachers and do *not* take it for granted that you'll be able to borrow or otherwise get hold of anything you're missing. It is your responsibility alone to make sure you have all of your stuff.

For most maths exams, 'everything' consists of:

- A transparent pencil case big enough for all of your stuff.
- A calculator, if you're allowed one. I recommend the Casio fx83 GT plus, but others are available[2]. Check

that a) you're allowed to bring a calculator and b) if you have a fancy-pants one (like a graphical calculator), make sure your exam board allows them.

- Several black-ink pens, all of which you've checked to make sure they're working.
- Several sharp pencils. I like to use mechanical pencils because I can see when they're running out, but there's nothing wrong with the old-fashioned sort.
- A rubber.
- A pencil sharpener, if you're using old-fashioned pencils. (The rest of us will just twist.)
- A geometry kit. Specifically, a pair of compasses that keep their width and a pencil that fits the hole; a protractor; and a ruler. They'll often have a stencil and some set-squares in, but these are of little use to anyone.

Note: some computer-based exams, such as teacher-training tests, don't allow you to take *anything* into the exam room. Check before you arrive!

One last thing: before you go into the exam, make sure your phone is off[3]. Phones ringing or buzzing in the exam hall are a major distraction, to you and to others. It's not just about manners, though, it's entirely conceivable that you could be disqualified if your phone rings mid-exam. Don't take the chance!

## *Cheat sheet*

Assuming you've made a cheat sheet, right before the exam is an ideal time to read through it. You're trying to get the facts on it into your short-term memory so you can regurgitate them onto an unobtrusive part of your exam paper the minute you're allowed to.

You want to make sure you know the *structure* of your sheet — there's a thing about triangles in the top left, in blue, then a green thing about surds just to its right, and so on — as well as the *content* — cover up the blue thing about triangles and make sure you can reel it off from memory.

Hopefully, you did the hard work yesterday of making it memorable, so today it's just a case of refreshing your memory and getting it down, quickly, onto the page when you're told to turn over your paper.

If you forget something? That's ok, let it go. Remembering stuff is hard, and if the things on the cheat sheet were obvious, you wouldn't have written them down. The important thing is to keep as much of it as you can in your memory, so that you can convert it into marks later.

## *Have a snack*

Exam halls are set up to minimise distractions. There's meant to be absolute silence, nothing on the walls to look at except maybe a clock, no phones — all of it to help you concentrate on your work.

That doesn't mean there are no distractions, though: common ones involve bodily functions (while it's ok to ask for a toilet break during an exam, it does eat into your available time; it's a very good idea to go before the start of the exam) and, especially, hunger and thirst.

Look, it's hard enough doing a maths exam under pressure at the best of times. Making it harder for yourself by skipping breakfast or going in dehydrated is just silly. What are you trying to achieve?

Before you go into the exam, make sure you've had enough food to see you through to the end — have an energy bar snack or something filling. It's not just about staving off the hunger pangs, it's also about making sure your brain has the fuel it needs to think straight. When you're hungry, your body responds by focussing on low-level, survival tasks rather than high-level thinking tasks like expanding and simplifying.

Exams aren't necessarily comfortable situations. Don't make them any more uncomfortable than they need to be.

# CHAPTER THREE

## *At the start*

The first few minutes of the exam are critical for setting yourself on the right course for the rest of it. If you get yourself into a fluster the minute you turn the page, you're going to struggle to recover before you're told to stop writing.

On the other hand, if you have a solid plan of how things are going to go down once the clock starts ticking, you're much more likely to have a good test.

It's tempting to get straight into the first question and knuckle down — in fact, that's probably the most common technique in exams, and it obviously works for some people — but I don't think it's the most efficient way to approach things: it's a bit like charging into a running race without knowing how far you have to run! If you're not careful, you'll wear yourself out in the first few miles, or (just as bad) treat the race with too much respect and find you're way off of your target time.

In this chapter, I offer some alternatives. Two of them (start with the easy marks, and start with the hard questions) are completely contradictory, and will work well for different students. I'd suggest looking at both and seeing what makes sense for you! However, the other two — read through the paper and plan your time — are both top-quality exam technique tips that ought to be mandatory.

## *Read the paper*

Before you do anything else, skim through the paper. Don't get bogged down in the detail of the questions, but read it carefully enough that you can say "that's a SOH CAH TOA question and I know how to do those" or "argh! Probability trees! That's going to take some thinking."

If you go through and put a smiley face next to the questions you're confident on, you'll get a sense of 'I know what I'm doing here', which is a much better frame of mind to be in than "oh God oh God oh God I'm going to fail."

There's a side benefit as well, though: if you read the hard questions before you tackle the easy ones, your subconscious starts working on those problems, dredging up details from the back of your mind so that they're... not *easy* when you get to them, but at least *less impossible*. Less impossible is good. Less impossible takes you from no idea to vague idea, from blank page to a few relevant lines, from no marks to one or two. Sometimes, less impossible becomes borderline possible or better.

Less impossible can be the difference between a D and a C, between resits and sixth form, between a job and a career.

Less impossible is your friend. Give it a chance to show up: read the paper first.

### *Low-hanging fruit*

For almost every student, I advise the 'low-hanging fruit' strategy for tackling exam papers. It boils down to:

**Do the easy stuff first**.

There are all sorts of good reasons for this, but the main ones are:

- You build up a head of steam and get some easy wins early on
- Once you've done the easy stuff and got the quick, cheap marks out of the way, you can assess how much time you have for the harder questions — often, you can take longer than you would originally have planned.
- The really important one: *you make sure you get the points for stuff you can do.* I can't count the number of students I've seen upset because they spent too long on a hard question without realising there were some give-aways later on.

Of course, I'll remind you that 'easy' is a subjective term — I have friends who can do advanced vector calculus in their heads, but struggle to add up. The paper is usually arranged from 'easy' to 'hard', but only in the examiner's head! It might well be that there are questions *easier for you* that come after questions you find difficult.

Make sure you give the 'easy' questions some respect, by checking your answer makes sense and spending a little time on them — the point of doing them first is to make sure you pick up all the marks you can, so make sure you pick up the marks!

### *Hard stuff first*

"Low-hanging fruit" isn't the only strategy for tackling an exam. (Obviously, there's the "do the questions in order" option, but who in their right minds would try that[4]?) One other alternative is the "hard stuff first" approach.

It's very unusual for me to recommend this strategy, as it's quite risky... unless you know you're a fast worker, and always have plenty of time left at the end of a test.

The main benefit of "hard stuff first" is that you get two bites at the hard questions: the initial attempt, when you're fresh, and — after you've had a shot at them and rattled off the easy questions, another chance to tackle them at the end, having had a bit of time for your subconscious to think the problems through.

This strategy isn't for everyone, by any means: like I say, you need to have a certain level of confidence in yourself, both in terms of speed and ability to pull it off. However, if you fit the bill, it might be worth trying. Let me know how you get on!

## *Plan your time*

Even before the start of the exam, you know:

- How long the test is; and
- How many marks are available.

You can use this information to work out how long you have, on average, for each mark (it's minutes divided by marks, just in case).

I'm not suggesting you use a stopwatch and say "I've done 1.2 minutes on this question, on to the next!", although that's definitely better than not looking at the clock at all. Instead, I suggest breaking the paper into three parts with roughly equal numbers of marks in each — and saying, if you've not reached the end of a part by the time you're a third of the way through the test, move on to the next part.

This isn't a perfect system (if you had more time available, you might experiment with splitting the test into six or eight bits instead), and you'll need to keep a bit of an eye on how time is progressing in each question, just so you avoid spending three minutes on a one-marker when you could use the time better elsewhere. However, it's better than no plan.

It's up to you how you manage your time, obviously. However you do it, it's preferable to have a plan than to come out saying "I spent too long on question 9 and didn't have time to finish." That's an inefficient way to do an exam, and will lower your result.

# CHAPTER FOUR

## *Mental management*

The spring of 1998 — I know, it was a long time ago — I was finishing my second year at university. I had, up until that point, been the kind of maths student you probably hate: absolutely sailing through, mocking disappointment at the occasional mark or two dropped, and generally dripping hubris.

Oh yes, the hubris.

The hubris meant I was entirely unprepared, both in a study sense and a mental sense, for my Analysis and Algebra exam. I turned over the paper and read the first question. I didn't immediately understand it. That was fine; I only needed to answer eight of the ten questions.

Second question? Nut-uh. This was beginning to get worrying.

Question 3? I thought: *I know how to spell some of those words.* My breathing got shallow. My eyes lost focus. I wanted to yell and cry (although, obviously, I was in an exam hall, so I couldn't.) My head started playing a loop of "You're going to fail, you're going to fail, you're going to fail."

This was not good. Looking back, this was probably the first time I suffered a panic attack, and it would be another decade before I finally figured out how to manage them properly. The advice that follows is hard-won, and definitely worth remembering when you find yourself going into meltdown in an exam — or anywhere else for that matter!

Tip: If you're suffering panic attacks, it's worth seeing your GP before they escalate — and consider paying for counselling. That's what finally got my head straightened out.

## *Breathe deeply*

There are several different types of fuel your brain relies on. The various proteins, fluids and other chemicals that support every part of your body help keep it going, for sure (which is why you should have a snack and something to drink before you go in to the exam), but just as important is the brain's supply of oxygen.

Am I really telling you that you need to breathe? You'd be quite entitled to yell "Are you sure, doctor? Is that what I've been doing wrong? I've looked for the solution until I'm blue in the face...", but do hear me out.

Pretend you've just run an uncomfortably long distance and breathe accordingly — shallow, panting breaths. Feel yourself tensing up? That's exactly what you don't want to do. Don't do that.

Instead, take a long, deep breath: really try to get the air down as far into your lungs as it'll go, all the way down to the bottom of your rib cage. Breathe slowly — count steadily to ten as you breathe in. See how much more relaxed and confident you feel already? Let the breath out, slowly, and repeat until your head is in the right place.

It sounds daft, doesn't it? If there's one thing you know how to do, without even thinking about it, it's breathing. That's what I thought, too. Until I tried it when I was about to go into a panic attack... which didn't materialise. Recognising I'm in a stressful situation and breathing accordingly has transformed my life — part of the problem with panic was that I didn't know what to do to control it.

Now I do. And so do you.

## *Sit up straight*

Not to get all sergeant-major or anything, but sit up straight! Stop slouching!

There are all sorts of benefits to looking after your posture (not least the fact that sitting up straight makes you less likely to come out with an aching back — although, admittedly, that's more of a problem when you're my age.) The two main ones you're interested in relate to confidence and (echoing the last section) breathing.

If you go into a random classroom, you can tell at a glance who are the attentive, engaged students and which ones just don't want to be there: guess what? It's all in the posture.

Your mind speaks body language. If you sit up straight, like the engaged students, your brain thinks "Oh! It's attention time. I'd better focus, stay alert, and be at my best." If you slouch like the others, your brain thinks "Meh, there's not much point, really, is there?"

Which of those is the attitude you need for the exam? Mhm, that's right.

In a nod to how things interrelate, it's also much easier to breathe well when you're sitting up straight: if you slouch, you're not giving your lungs much room to fill with air, so your breathing is a little restricted. If you're sitting up as if you own the room, you can take deep, full breaths and make sure you're getting plenty of oxygen.

## *Positive talk*

I'm writing this during Wimbledon (summer is the quiet season for teaching) and the commentators are making a big thing about 'self-talk' — players yelling 'come on!' and telling themselves to focus, rather than things like "I'm going to lose" or "I'm rubbish at tennis". Players that talk positively to themselves have a significant edge over the players that talk negatively — or who whine to the umpire, or who bark at the ball-girls.

What goes for tennis, in this case, goes just as much for exams. If you say "I'm rubbish at maths, I can't do this", you're probably going to prove yourself right. There are more constructive messages you can give yourself, such as:

- "This might be hard, but I'm smart: I can figure it out."
- "Help me out, brain — I know we've covered this, it's in there somewhere."
- "I might not be able to see it right now, but I'll come back to it later on and crack it then."

You don't (I hope) choose to hang out with people who are continually putting you down; it's much more fulfilling to be around people who compliment you and build you up. There's a name for people in that first kind of group: they're bullies. If you continually put yourself down, you're being bullied (which isn't ideal) and you're being a bully (which is worse).

Stand up for yourself against your own bullying. Be strong. Be positive.

You can do it. See?

## *Stretch your muscles*

Obviously, you can't get up in the exam and walk about — but you can do a few stretches to get your blood flowing and stave off the pins and needles for a bit.

Three simple stretches you can do without drawing much, if any, attention to yourself:

- **Legs**. Reach one of your legs out in front of you and point your toes. You should feel it in the back of your thigh and the bottom of your foot. Hold it for a few seconds, and then change legs.
- **Back**. Put your left hand on your right shoulder and your right hand on your left shoulder, crossing your arms. Without moving your head, twist your torso so it's facing to the left; you should feel this in your lower back. Twist back the other way so your torso is facing right, then back to face the front.
- **Shoulders**. Sit slightly forwards and try to touch your elbows behind your back. Unless you're incredibly flexible, you won't get anywhere near, but you'll feel the tension in your chest and shoulders — this one always makes me feel more wide awake!

With all stretches, do them fairly gently and don't bounce; a sure-fire way of drawing attention to yourself is to be rolling around complaining about pulled muscles!

I find that taking a quick, unobtrusive stretch can be a

good way to 'reset' my brain and let me approach things with a fresh mind.

## *Swear like a sailor*

The best thing you can possibly do in an exam is to stand on your chair and yell "*yo ho [redacted] ho!*" at the top of your voice.

No, wait, that's about the worst thing. My bad. (That said, a friend of mine did once stand up in an exam, point out of the window, shout "*it's snowing!*" and sit down as if nothing had happened. I do not advise this.)

However, swearing *in your head* or *very quietly under your breath* is quite a subversive way to release some tension. You can mentally insert bad words into the questions. You can imagine visiting untold horrors on whichever moron they've picked to survey their classmates in *this* paper. You can curse all the examiners to Hull and back.

Don't get too distracted with creative insults and ferocious swears — one, because it's easy to let it get out of control and turn into a Mr/Ms Mutter who gets aggressively shushed, and two because it's meant to be a way of clearing your mind a little to help you focus on the actual question, and if you're wondering which is the most offensive thing you can say about Kate the photographer, you're not thinking about solving the [redacted] question.

**Tip**: be really careful to swear at the paper and the examiner rather than yourself. *You're* smart, remember, and *you* can do it.

# CHAPTER FIVE

## *Approach*

The two big keys to exam success are how you prepare for the exam, and how you approach it once you're in there. This chapter is about that approach — how you set yourself up mentally to do well.

I've noticed certain common threads among the attitudes of students who do well, and among the students who do poorly. The more successful students are analytical, approaching unfamiliar questions with a spirit of 'I wonder how to do this' and generally take a can-do approach to their work.

By contrast, students who say "I've never seen this before" and throw down their pens, who make excuses, who find ways *not* to do their work... they tend not to get as good grades.

Big surprise, eh? Well, we all know that correlation doesn't imply causation, but there's a pretty strong link here. Now, the question is, how can you become the kind of student with a positive attitude (what this year's trend calls a 'growth mindset', but will doubtless be known as something else by the time you read this)? How can you get rid of the negative habits of the mind that stop you from going at it full steam ahead?

## No excuses

You want another example of an attitude that distinguishes students who tend to do well from those that struggle? It's to do with how they talk before the paper.

Going through some exercises, the two students may come across something they find difficult. The thriving student says "Oh! That's interesting — I'd better practise that a bit more." The struggling student says "Let's hope that doesn't come up in the real exam."

Revision strategies based on hope and prayer are about as effective as closing your eyes to make the monster go away. Put more harshly, you're making excuses not to do the work, and your exam result will suffer as a consequence.

(An aside: candidates who expect to do well, if they're going to hope for anything, should hope for a difficult paper; it will allow them to show what they can do, while benefiting from lower grade boundaries.)

In *this* book, we don't make excuses, and we don't run away from the stuff we're meant to know. We think about what we'll do if the situation arises, so we're prepared if it does. Even if it's a case of "here are some things I could write down if I'm put on the spot", you need to have a strategy for dealing with the topics you don't want to deal with.

In general, excuses are poisonous. Anyone can find reasons for why they didn't do well — I missed a few classes, we had six different teachers, I moved school, the kids in class muck about, I get hay-fever... the list is endless. The trouble is, when you get your exam certificate back, it doesn't say "E (but he moved schools, so it's ok)" or "D (not bad considering the school she was at)". It says "E" or "D", and you'll probably need to resit if you want to get into sixth form or go into a professional career.

In summary: kill the excuses before they kill your dreams.

### *Treat it as a game*

A game? Surely an exam is far too serious to treat as a game? Well, maybe. But there's a school of thought that says games are serious business: for example, "Football isn't a matter of life and death," said former Liverpool manager Bill Shankly, "it's more important than that." Game theory, a fairly modern development in maths, has led to several Nobel Prizes (although largely in Economics, which is the Nobel Prize that doesn't really count).

How do I mean, treat it as a game? I mean a quiz kind of game, the kind of game where you're asked questions and score points by giving correct answers. Put like that, it's not so far-fetched, is it?

I know that a maths exam quiz game is hardly anyone's idea of fun, but thinking of it in those terms is a powerful way to take the edge off. Rather than think of some anonymous Demon Headmaster figure evilly writing the questions down, imagine it being read out in Alexander Armstrong's voice. Rather than treating it as a horrible test, think of it as some sort of weird social event where you're not allowed to talk to anyone until afterwards, when you can compare answers and speculate on how you did.

When you treat it as a game, you can start coming up with strategies to help you win — how can I pick up another couple of points here? What can I do to get Richard Osman saying "that's a terrific answer" rather than "bad luck, I can see what you were thinking"?

You can even hum the theme tune of your favourite quiz show on the way into the exam. Who's going to know it's you?

## *Pick up marks*

One minor improvement you can make to how you think about exams is to change your thinking about marks from "look at how many I've dropped" to "look at how many I've picked up."

This changes your thinking from a defensive "oh crap, I'd better not make mistakes — I'll leave that blank" to "If I try something, I might pick up a mark or two."

I've talked elsewhere about not leaving things blank if you can possibly help it — there are some students who seem to think that leaving it blank isn't really getting it wrong, that somehow if you don't give an answer, it doesn't count.

That's idiotic. Don't be like them.

If you leave a question blank, you automatically get no marks for it, just as if you'd written "I am a fish" repeatedly. You will pick up no marks. That is bad. Don't do it.

The marks on the paper are there for you to pick up: you start the paper with zero and get your score by answering questions. You have no marks to drop, only marks to gain.

Tricks like going back and checking your work are ways to pick up extra marks, not defence against dropping them. You cannot lose what you do not have to begin with.

Gosh, this has all gone a bit philosophical. With that, I hope you have become enlightened.

## *Play down the stakes*

One of the many secrets about maths exams is this: if you do poorly, you don't actually die. In fact, you don't suffer any physical harm at all; the only real damage is a slightly bruised ego.

Obviously, you don't want to do poorly, you want to get the best possible grade and go on to the next stage of whatever you want to do without hindrance. *But*, however much your teachers and parents have been stressing to you that these Really Important Exams will Decide Your Future, the truth is that falling short isn't the end of the world. It's an inconvenience, but it's not a calamity.

In almost all cases, if your results aren't up to what you need, you're able to resit the exams later in the year, or next summer. That's a pain, and it'd be better all round to do all right first time around, but there is a safety net. That's an important thing to realise. Why?

Because, if your mental energy stops going into the pit of "I'm going to fail and my life will be *over*!" but rather into "hm, simultaneous equations, what can I do with these?", you're going to study much more effectively, pick up more marks, and generally kick more posterior than if you're in a panicked tizzy.

If you mentally reduce what's at stake in your exam, you'll be less tense, more receptive to learning, and find it easier to cope with the rest of the stress that comes with exam season.

Tip: not all stress is bad stress. A little bit of adrenaline is a good thing, and helps you think more quickly; it's when it becomes overpowering that things go badly . It's up to you to find the right balance!

# CHAPTER SIX

## *Problem-solving strategies*

I'm writing this in the aftermath of the 'Hannah's sweets' furore. The 2015 GCSE maths paper had a question that wasn't precisely in the form students had seen probability questions before, and some — or rather many — were unhappy about it. What business had EdExcel in setting *new styles* of question? (Never mind that there's a similar, indeed harder, question in the 2004 paper.) Let me put this violin down.

I thought Hannah's sweets was a good question: it differentiates between students who can think on their feet, so to speak, and those who can recognise and regurgitate methods. That's not to disparage the R&R crowd, those are valuable skills — but they're not the skills of an A/A* mathematician, any more than someone who can spew out memorised essay answers in an English exam is an A/A* candidate in that subject.

The question rewarded candidates who were ready to have a stab at it. To try something out. To treat it as a puzzle.

That's what this chapter is about: looking at ways you can tackle questions as a puzzle. What tactics and strategies can you employ when you're not really sure what you have to do? It's not about playing the system to pick up cheap marks (don't worry, I cover that elsewhere), it's about solving problems on the fly.

Incidentally, that's a skill that will serve you well long beyond your exam.

## *Draw a picture*

Obviously, drawing a picture or a diagram doesn't always make a lot of sense — if you're doing a purely arithmetical or algebraic question, there's unlikely to be much a picture can add (although sometimes algebra with pictures is easier to see than algebra with letters. But I digress).

If you're doing a geometrical problem, though, a picture is usually a good idea. Even if there's a picture given to you on the paper, drawing it out yourself forces you to focus on the various different parts of it and how they fit together.

I recommend drawing BIG — I had a teacher who insisted that anything smaller than half a page didn't count as a diagram. I don't go quite that far, but the bigger you draw, the more room you have to label things, and the less likely you are to confuse yourself by squashing things together.

Drawing uses different parts of your brain to arithmetic and algebra — sometimes, it's just the jolt you need to get yourself unstuck!

**Tip**: Sometimes, even doing a little doodle completely unrelated to the question can get you unstuck — but don't fall into the trap of doodling as an avoidance strategy!

Don't worry about drawing accurately or nicely (your exam paper isn't going in the National Gallery when it's finished, it's going into a scanner and then probably into a shredder, after being seen by maybe a handful of people — so it's ok for it to be scrappy. As long as *you* can read and understand it, it's absolutely fine.

**Tip**: most GCSE papers have one or several "blank pages" at the back of the paper. Leaving aside the philosophical conundrum of a blank page having something written on them to show that they're blank, these are a great place to put any extra working, big pictures, and things you're trying to remember.

## *Is there a variable?*

Look. If a question gives you an $x$-value and an equation with an $x$ in it, and you say "I've no idea where to start", you're not trying.

If all else fails, try mushing stuff together. If I put this value in the equation, what happens? Does that look like a sensible answer to the question? Well then, it's already better than leaving it blank.

Similarly, if there's something you don't know — a length, an angle, a value — try giving it a name. $x$ is traditional, but you can call it anything you like. What do you know about $x$? How does it fit with values you do know? How does it fit with values you *don't* know? Can you make an equation out of them?

Again, the process of trying to mash these things together sometimes flukes you a few marks by accidentally getting something that's part of the real solution;

sometimes it even gives you a brainwave and gets you all the way to the real solution.

Explore! If you've got time — and presumably, you have time, or else you'd be doing the easy questions — don't worry too much about right or wrong, just see if there's something you can get hold of.

## What constraints do you have?

In other words, what do you know about the answer you're trying to find? Are you expecting a whole number? A fraction? Must it be positive? Is there an upper bound to it? Is it a measurement? An angle? An algebraic expression?

What else do you know? If it's a geometry problem, can you put some limits on the size of your answer? If it's a triangle, the last side can't be longer than the two other sides. If you've got a weird shape to find the area of, can you find the area of a box that encloses it? Your answer has to be smaller than that.

(Aside: if gap between your shape and that box leaves you with a shape that's easy to find the area of, then you've found a short-cut to the answer. Well done.)

If it's algebra, what things do you expect to see? If you're drawing a graph, what ought it to look like? Do the readings in your table have to add up to a particular number?

(This last one, incidentally, is a good way of catching mistakes — if you've got a point or a bar or something that looks out of place, the chances are you've made a mistake. The good news is, ta-da! You can put it right!)

If there's a picture, even one that's not accurately drawn, can you get an estimate for the right answer by eyeballing it?

By putting constraints on what your answer can be, you're a) eliminating possible wrong answers, and b) thinking about the question in a way that can move you towards the answer.

# CHAPTER SEVEN

## *Write in clear, correct sentences*

"But it's *maths*, not *English!*" you protest. Or, probably, "but its maths not english LOL".

Let's get one thing clear: mathematical writing is a language. A beautiful, concise, idiosyncratic language. It's important that you write your maths correctly, but more to the point, you need to explain it to other people — or else it looks like gibberish. Try it! Go and look back to some exercise you did six months ago. Does it make any sense?

If you're a computer programmer, you'll know about the idea of documenting your code — making sure you (or whoever comes to look at your program in the future) know what you were thinking and what it's supposed to do.

Doing this with your maths will make you a hero to your examiner. It enables them to see what you're thinking, and in some cases to give you marks for method even if you've messed up the sums completely. More to the point, it marks you out as "one of us" — someone who understands the importance of helping others understand their work.

If you're going to write, though, write *clearly* and *correctly*. While examiners are likely to overlook the odd misplaced apostrophe or capital letter, you're trying to sell yourself as something like a professional — if you're going to a job interview, you don't show up scruffy, and you make sure your CV is neatly printed on good-quality paper; you make sure you present as good a side of yourself as you possibly can.

Your exams are (arguably) more important than a job interview. In many cases, they can be the thing that *gets* you a job interview. So, do yourself a favour: smarten up your work and take care over the details. You'll come across much better!

## *Handwriting*

Picture the scene, dear reader: a dark garret, somewhere dismal like Maidenhead or Bicester. A teacher, 'fresh' from a day of riot control with her year sevens, wearily turns on her computer: she has exam marking to do. Lots of it. Dozens upon dozens of scripts, from all across the country, scanned and digitised for her to go through.

In among this digital pile lie your answers to your maths exam. She rubs her bleary eyes, refills her coffee, and sees your messy scrawl in front of her.

Now, put yourself in her shoes: is she more likely to a) take several minutes looking at your work from several different angles in a desperate attempt to figure out what exactly you meant, and reward your obscurity accordingly, or b) say 'I can't read that' and give you no marks?

If you said a), try again.

If you said a) again, try again but say something different this time.

Your exam script doesn't need to be a work of illuminated calligraphy that deserves to be carefully preserved in the British Museum under ideal lighting conditions — but it does need to be legible, and it does need to be clear.

I know it's a bit late in the day to be working on your

handwriting, but if you give an answer, read it back and think "I'm not sure that's easy to read", consider writing it out again underneath *before* crossing out the original. (As you'll see shortly, that's the correct order to do things in.)

## *Distinguish your letters*

I have a terrible habit of writing 5s that look like Ss. I don't write the top of the five straight and flat like I ought to and it leads to me making mistakes (and, worse, writing things down unclearly so my students can't understand what's going on).

I know it's a bit late in the day to be worrying about how you write letters (presumably, the way you've written letters since you were about six) — but there are things you can do to make the odd letters clearer and less susceptible to being misread — either by you or by the examiner. Here are some of the common ones to get confused:

- 2 and z. I cross my zs so they don't get confused with 2.
- u and v. I make sure to put a tail on my u and a little flourish at the top of my v (a little like a short square root sign).
- x and ×. It's best just not to use × for multiplication

(brackets are much better) — unless you're doing some sort of vector maths that requires a cross product. In any case, writing your x as two back-to-back semicircles means you won't mix them up.

- b and 6; q and 9. Again, giving the letters definite tails and curving your numbers appropriately will keep these distinct.
- t and +. Once more, put a tail at the bottom of your t.
- s and 5. Do as I say, not as I do. Make the top of your 5 flat.
- l and 1 and I. Tough one, this: again, a tail on your lower-case l will do the trick, possibly writing it with a definite curl; capital I should have serifs at the top and bottom (so it looks like a sort of sideways H, but not so stretched out); number 1 should have a serif at the bottom and a flourish at the top.
- B and 8. Straight left edge to the B.

Are there any I've missed? Let me know!

## *Layout*

I'm not an examiner. I have no desire to be an examiner. But I have seen the kinds of answers students turn in on mock papers.

Excuse me a minute. I need a little cry.

Bits of working scattered all over the page. No explanation of what the sums mean or what they're trying to work out. Maybe, eventually, an answer on the answer line.

It's madness, I tell you. Madness.

Laying out your work neatly and logically is a), an enormous chore. I recognise that. It's also b) much easier for you to read back and find mistakes in, and c) much easier for an examiner to follow.

If you're doing trial and improvement, for heaven's sake use a table. If you're doing a 'which deal is better?' question, split the page into two or three columns and say things like:

total cost = £80
5% of £80 = £4
£80 - £4 = £76

... in each of them.

Make the examiner's life easy by explaining to them what you're doing. The easier you make it for them to give you marks, the more marks you're going to get. It really is as simple as that.

## *Don't cram it in*

Related to layout, when I was doing my A-levels (wibbly-screen flashback), there was one kind of question that I'd *always* lose marks on — the binomial distribution, which you don't care about yet. I'd lose marks because I tried to write it out as

$$(2+x)^{-2} = (2^{-2})\left(1+\frac{x}{2}\right)^{-2} = \left(\frac{1}{4}\right)\left[1+(-2)\left(\frac{x}{2}\right)+\frac{(-2)(-3)}{2}\left(\frac{x}{2}\right)^2+\frac{(-2)(-3)(-4)}{6}\left(\frac{x}{2}\right)^3+\right.$$

... and keep going across the page. I'd inevitably run out of space, cram my work up, be unable to read it back, lose a minus sign, and get the wrong answer. I didn't learn any better until several years later, when I realised it was ok to write:

$$1 \quad = \quad 1$$

$$-2 \qquad \left(\frac{x}{2}\right) \quad = \quad (-2)\left(\frac{x}{2}\right)$$

$$\frac{(-2)(-3)}{2} \quad \left(\frac{x}{2}\right)^2 \quad = \quad (3)\left(\frac{x^2}{4}\right)$$

$$\frac{(-2)(-3)(-4)}{6} \quad \left(\frac{x}{2}\right)^3 \quad = \quad (-4)\left(\frac{x^3}{8}\right)$$

... instantly much easier to see what was going on and to

fit everything onto the page without running into space issues. (It also, incidentally, gave me an insight into some of the patterns, but that's a completely different story).

The moral of this story: have a look at where you're about to write. If there's not enough space across the way, split it into several lines. That's allowed. If there's not enough space vertically, turn over the page. (I appreciate this isn't possible in some exams. In that case, try making columns. But not too narrow, or you'll run out of space across the way).

Always give yourself room to write clearly.

# CHAPTER EIGHT

### *Getting unstuck*

It happens to everyone: you're aware that there are words on the page, you may even be able to read them — but they're just not fitting together into anything that makes any sort of sense. Your mind is blank, except for the part that generates face-saving excuses like "I've never covered this before" or "Maybe I was away that day."

First up, kill the excuses. Finding 'reasons' you can't do something is a great way to ensure it doesn't happen. Unfortunately, that tends to lower your exam scores considerably. It's much better to approach it from a point of view of "I'm smart, I've studied some maths, I should be able to work this out."

That's the thing, you see: a maths exam isn't quite a quiz, or a memory test (although some of the questions might look that way); it's a test of thinking, of working things out, of *trying* things out, of perseverance.

If I had a penny for every time I'd heard a student say "I didn't know so I left it blank!", I'd be... well, slightly better off than I am. If I had two pence for every time one of these students got it right, when asked to tackle it for a second time with me not letting them give up, I'd have yet more money.

I know, I know: a maths exam is a high-pressure situation (see: kill the excuses) and it's not always easy to think things through. Perhaps, like most good mathematicians, you're lazy. This chapter is your chance to sit back, put the blunt end of your pen in your mouth, and do a bit of thinking in an effort to get yourself unstuck.

## *What do you know?*

The first thing to do when faced with a seemingly impossible question is to ask: what do I know?

There are two types of knowledge that can help you here: first, and most important, is things you are told in the question. Usually, if you have a big block of text, the facts and details contained within it are important for getting to the answer. This type of knowledge includes stuff on the formula sheet — it's worth having a quick skim of that to see if there's anything at all relevant to your situation!

The second type of knowledge is what you've brought with you. Are there any equations, formulas or techniques you can bring to bear on it? What can you dredge up from your mathematical past that seems relevant?

Start with a brainstorm of all of the stuff you know that seems relevant, and start grouping it together into things you can combine.

Tip: Don't worry about whether you're doing things the most efficient way — if you're genuinely stuck, perfect is the enemy of good. Any method that gets the right answer is (usually) a perfectly fine one to employ. (The only exception to that is if you're explicitly told the method to use, or if you're told a method you mustn't use. In either case, do what you're told.)

But sometimes, writing everything down doesn't magically point you to the correct answer. What then?

### *Keep going*

I think it was Churchill (the prime minister, not the dog) who said something like: when you're going through hell, keep going. It's almost a cliché, but only because it's good advice.

When I'm not writing books to help people like your good self through their exams, I'm generally teaching people like you in person to try to help them through *their* exams, so I see people getting stuck quite a lot.

One thing I've noticed: if, rather than saying "well, now you do this", I say "keep at it — what might you try?", nine times out of ten my student comes up with a great idea. They weren't really stuck, they just needed to think a little longer. I joke about getting a "what would Colin ask?" wristband for them to toy with when they feel stuck.

They, like you, know more than they think they do, and just lack the self-belief to push through the moment of "what now?"

It's ok to feel confused and/or stuck. Stop for a moment. Take a breath. Chew on your pen lid. Think about what you might try next. Even if it's the wrong thing, it's better than leaving it blank.

### *Can you talk it through*

In an exam, sadly, you can't tap your pal on the shoulder and discuss the intricate details of the tricky problem in front of you. This is one of the big problems I have with exams.

However, there's nothing to stop you having an *imaginary* conversation with your brainy friends, your tutor or that guy off of Khan Academy[5]. Quietly, in your head, come up with specific questions for them and imagine what they'd say. Would they ask you questions back? What would they tell you to do? What would they need to know so that they could solve the problem?

Once you've got precise questions for your imaginary friends, and precise answers from them, bingo! You're three-quarters of the way to answering the question yourself.

Imagining what someone else would say is a good way of remembering things you might otherwise have forgotten. One of the biggest bonuses of having smart friends (apart from, you know, smart friends being awesome) is that their smartness can rub off on you.

**Tip**: In my GCSE maths class, whenever a difference of two squares questions came up, my teacher would pick on a girl called Becky to answer it. It seemed ridiculous, almost unfair. We'd take the mickey out of it: when *we* saw a difference of two squares question, we started saying "Becky?" And then, when it came up in the exam, every one of us recognised the kind of question straight away and answered it without problems. Associating your friends with tricky kinds of problem — and their answers — is a good way to keep things remembered!

## *Turn it upside down*

This sounds a little bit out there, but bear with me: try looking at the question from a (literal) different angle. Does the picture give any more clues when you look at it sideways-on? If you try to read the question upside-down, does anything jump out at you?

Possibly not. There are no guarantees in the crazy world of getting unstuck. But sometimes, just sometimes, doing something that seems ridiculous is enough to jolt your brain out of its funk and get it churning into motion again.

(You can do all sorts of weird things in the same vein — imagine you're sitting, nice and relaxed in your favourite comfy chair, or at the stadium watching the football when the manager wanders over and says "we need you to solve this, or we're going to be relegated[6]", or sitting at the beach looking out to sea. Mentally change your location, and see if it helps change your mental state at all.)

As I say, no promises. But it's worth a try.

### *Experimental approach*

If you're absolutely stuck, and you have plenty of time, there's nothing wrong with trying a few guesses to see if you can get close to the right answer. If you're smart about it, you can use your guesses to narrow down what the solution ought to be: for example, you can use your trial and improvement knowledge to get progressively closer to the answer.

You need to be a wee bit careful about the experimental approach because trial and improvement isn't always a method that gets marks, especially if you're told *not* to use it. However, once you know the answer, you can sometimes work backwards to find the steps you needed to take.

**Tip:** going about maths experimentally, especially in an

exam, is usually less efficient than working things out systematically. However, when you're so stuck you can't see a systematic way, experiments can be an ok alternative.

## *Come back to it later*

The last suggestion for getting unstuck is probably the most obvious of them all: just let it go. Come back to it later on if you get the chance.

That's not as "just give up" as it sounds — while your brain is off looking at other questions, your mind is quietly ticking over, wondering how to close the unclosed loop. When you come back to it later, sometimes — not always[7] — you'll find that something has clicked into place.

There are things you can do to improve your chances of this. For example, most of the suggestions in this chapter involve thinking quite hard, reading in some detail, looking from all angles — all of these are things that get the structure and detail of the question into your head so your subconscious can muck about with it while you do something more productive. By contrast, if you just glance at it and say "nope, can't do it", you're not giving yourself much of a chance.

**Tip:** put a big star next to a question you've left unfinished. This makes it easier to find when you remember to come back to it.

Some glorious days, you'll be midway through another question when your brain suddenly says "HANG ON! It's *easy!*" and you can go back to fill in the details. Everyone should experience that at least once. If you're lucky, it'll be in your exam.

# CHAPTER NINE

## *Mark-winning tactics*

Obviously, the best way to get a good score in an exam is to know the material inside out, and have done so many past papers that you know what each question is almost before you read it, and to be in top mental shape at exactly the right time.

No, me either.

In practice, one of the best ways to give your grade a quick boost is by playing the game: looking at how you can cynically and deliberately pick up marks even when you don't know the answer or very much about the topic. This chapter looks at some of those.

It doesn't specifically look at tactics for avoiding dropping marks — things like making sure your answer answers the question and administrative details like 'give your answer to three decimal places' or 'give your answer in terms of π'. Instead, this is about picking up marks that you otherwise would have thrown away without a fight.

Some of it, you might think, is simple common sense. But you'd be surprised how uncommon common sense really is: for every person who says "people really do that?!" when I suggest these basic exam technique no-nos, there are two who actually do.

## *No crossing-out*

"I wrote that!" A brief pause. "But then I crossed it out."

"Did you write something else?"

"No, I left it blank."

Dear readers, I don't think there's a jury in the land who would have found me guilty of murder.

Why? Why, for the love of God, would you cross out an answer if you didn't have anything better to write?

Repeat after me: **there is no situation[8] where a question left blank outscores something written.**

If your answer is wrong, you gain no marks by crossing it out. If it was right — or even merit-worthy — you lose any marks you might have picked up. Don't cross things out.

With one exception: if you think your answer is wrong, by all means try to work out a better one — but don't cross your original work out until you've reached the end of your correction. If you must cross something out, do it neatly, with a ruler. This is as much for speed reasons as for neatness — but I don't know of any examiners who like to see heavily-scribbled-out work.

Generally, crossing out your work is shooting yourself in the foot at point-blank range. You should always leave unfinished and possibly incorrect work intact, unless you have already written down a better answer.

## Make a start

When I was a researcher, struggling to motivate myself to do anything, I had a message written on my whiteboard:

*Set aside your fears and make a small, imperfect start.*

It's still my best advice for anyone who doesn't know where to start. Don't worry about getting it wrong, or looking daft, or anything else — just see what you can get down. Copy out the critical bits of the questions. See if there's an equation you can write down from somewhere. See if there are two bits of information you can combine. See if there's a length or an angle you can find. See if you can tidy something up, or something you can make messier. See if there's something you can translate into maths.

It doesn't matter *what* you try. Trying *something* is the important thing. If it doesn't work out? Pity. If it does? Hello, bonus marks!

If it does, also, you've *started*. And once you've started, you can carry on a bit further. And a bit further.

Don't be frightened of hard questions — with a bit of thought, there's always something you can make a start on. And you should.

### *Anything from earlier*

Another frustrating conversation I often have with

students goes:

Student: "I didn't see how to do the first bit, so I skipped it."

Me: "But you did the second part, right?"

Student: "No, I figured if I couldn't do the first part..."

Me: "Did you read it?"

Student: *why would I do a thing like that look*

Me: *head, meet desk*

Exam questions are often structured in a way that allows you to carry on with the question even if you didn't get the first bit — typically the first part says "Show that (this thing) simplifies to (this other thing)" or similar. "Show that" is the key phrase; it means that the thing you're asked to show is true.

The second part with then say "Hence, or otherwise, (do something)." *Hence* is a really helpful word: it means "the thing you just worked out will help you." *Or otherwise* means you're free to do the something any way you fancy, but the simplest way is probably to use what you've just been told.

*Hence* questions give you the green light to carry on, even when you can't do the first bit. (You can come back to that later, if you want to.)

Similarly, later parts of the same question might be completely independent of the first bit and ask for something you do know.

Whatever you do, don't assume that just because you can't see a way in to part a), that parts b), c) and d) are impossible.

Another way to use details from earlier in the question is to look back at the information you're given and see what you haven't used. It's unusual for them to give you details you don't need (except story-telling details like someone's name or whatever ridiculous pseudocontext they're using to shoehorn this question in as an 'applied' one) — how can you fit any other facts in with what you've already worked out?

# CHAPTER TEN

## *At the end*

There are some students who are usually still writing when the call comes to "put your pens down, please". Most people, though, end up with a few minutes left at the end of the exam.

You have a couple of choices of how you can spend the time at the end of your paper. You can try to occupy your mind by counting ceiling tiles, or finding the prime factors of your best friend's phone number (what's that? Just me? Oh.)

Or, you can use the last few minutes to wring out a few more marks from your brain. As I keep saying: sometimes an extra mark is all you need to get your score past a grade boundary, and that can be the difference between one sixth form and another, or between never doing another maths exam and resits.

A third option is to put a few moments into stress control, by trying to make the wait for your results just a tiny bit less agonising. Most of the fear in opening the envelope[9] comes from not knowing what to expect. You have a chance to put that right!

## *Check answers*

If you're not still writing when you're told to stop, you have time to check your answers. This is dull.

However, as with anything else in this book, getting an extra mark can make an enormous difference — and it's no duller than sitting and daydreaming while the clock runs down.

There are two main kinds of answer-checking: the 'is this roughly right' kind and 'does this answer work?' kind.

To find out if something is roughly right, you can ask yourself whether your answer makes sense. If you do the same sum with everything rounded to one significant figure, do you get a similar answer? If you're doing a geometry problem, are your distances and angles a plausible size? (The diagrams may not be drawn accurately, but they're not drawn *that* badly — you should be able to eyeball what the numbers ought to be.) Have you avoided all of the booby-traps your teacher warned you about?

To find out whether an answer works, try putting it back into the original question. This is especially useful in algebra (for example, if you have an answer for a simultaneous equation, replacing x and y with your answers should make the equations true — otherwise, you've gone wrong.)

There are other ways to check your work, too: for example, if you have plenty of time, you can work the whole thing through in a different way, and check that you get the same answer.

If your answers check out, all well and good — if not, you need to decide how best to fix them. Remember: don't cross anything out until you have something better written down!

## *Estimate your score*

At the very end of your exam, assuming again that you're not still writing, take five minutes to make your summer a bit more peaceful, and work out what you think you've scored. (You can combine this with checking your answers if you want to.)

It's a simple process: go through, question by question, saying "that's definitely right — three marks" or "I've got a 50-50 chance of getting those two marks, so I'll call it one". Add them all up and remember this number. Be conservative, and tend to round borderline marks down.

This is unlikely to be *exactly* the score you get when you look at your results in August, but it ought to serve as a decent guide. When you get home, you can compare it to typical grade boundaries in previous years and say "unless I've completely misjudged it, that was probably a B" or "I think it was borderline B/C" — in any case, it takes away a little bit of the uncertainty.

If you've had a good paper, it's reassuring to be able to say "that went well, I might get an A if things fall right"; if it's not gone so well, it's better to know that early so you're not just fretting about what might be — instead, you can start planning about how you can work around it, or do better next time.

# CHAPTER ELEVEN

## *Afterwards*

What possible difference can you make after the exam?

Well, that's kind of the point: after the exam, you've done all you can do, and no amount of finger-crossing, second-guessing or petition-signing is going to make a blind bit of difference to your result. The 'afterwards' bit is all about how to manage your summer so you don't go crazy worrying about your result.

Because yes, it's important to get a good grade. Yes, your results have an impact on what happens next in your education or work career. Yes, it's understandable to be worried and stressed about them — although you might want to have a look at mentally de-escalating the stakes so you don't get over-wrought. (However you get on: someone, somewhere, has had a worse day than you. Almost certainly, someone has had a worse set of exam results, but more to the point, someone, somewhere, has been forced out of her home by a civil war, someone has got to the front of the food queue in the refugee camp just as they ran out of their meagre supplies, and someone has had to swim back to shore after the boat they were trying to escape on capsized. Just to put your day into context.)

Apart from comparing your potential plight with other people's, there are concrete things you can do to keep the post-exam worry from taking over your life, which boil down to:

- Don't whine;
- Don't disasterise; and
- Remember your estimate

These three things won't guarantee you sleep the sleep of the just, but they'll go a long way towards fending off the insomnia of the just terrified.

## *Don't whine*

It seems to be almost a rite of passage these days: you come out of an exam, say "that was really hard, I don't think I got a single mark", then go home and add whingey subtitles to a Hitler *Downfall* video. Or use some other meme to show how unfair and unreasonable it was for the exam board, in an exam testing whether you know the syllabus, to ask questions relating to the syllabus. Perhaps you sign a petition asking for an investigation into maths questions containing maths.

I strongly suggest not doing this.

It might make you feel a bit better about the exam, for a moment, maybe foster a sense of community about the outrages perpetrated upon you — but it's not going to change anything, and it'll mark you out as a *whiner*.

When you come around to applying for jobs, any recruiter worth their salt is going to look back through your social media profiles. If they see Sean Bean under your name saying "One does not simply SOLVE an exam question", they'll think: "oh. They're one of *those* people."

Employers want people who take responsibility for things, not blame other people for their misfortune. Grumbling about the hardness of exams, especially in public forums, is a great way of showing you're not the kind of employee they're looking for.

Plus, you're living up to the stereotype of an entitled

teenager, and who wants to live up to that?

## *Don't disasterise*

While the perils of whining about your exam in public are obvious, whining to yourself and your friends and family isn't all that much more helpful.

**Once you're out of the exam, there's nothing you can do.**

Complaining won't change anything.

Worrying won't change anything.

Saying "But what if...?" won't change anything — unless you're coming up with a fallback plan, just in case things don't go the way you hoped.

A fallback plan is a good thing, as it gives you a clear path, whether it's to go to sixth-form college, get a job, study for resits... as long as you have a plan B so you know that things will be OK even in your worst-case outcome, you won't waste your summer full of nerves about how your exams went.

If you find yourself thinking "but what if I get, like, 10%?", it's a good idea to remember what you estimated your score was. It may be off by a little bit, but it's likely to be a good anchor for you — try saying "I'm sure I did enough to get a B, but a C wouldn't be a disaster if I overestimated" (or similar) to keep the worries at bay.

I'm going to repeat something one last time to finish the book, as it's probably the most important thing for your post-exam mental health:

**Things will be OK, even in the worst case**.

However bad things get, there's always a way forward. The world doesn't end with a bad exam, just like world peace isn't achieved by a good one. If things don't go to plan, that's inconvenient — but there's always another plan.

## *Thanks*

I'd like to thank Hannah Coutts and Nathan Day for their helpful comments on the manuscript.

---

[1] Presumably. If you were excited about it, I don't think

you'd have picked this up.

[2] I've heard good things about the Casio fx991 ES Plus, too: especially if you're planning to go on to do A-level, the advanced functions can take a lot of weight off of your shoulders.

[3] Some schools don't allow phones anywhere near the exam hall.

[4] I have, under pressure, used the related "start at the back" technique in one exam, but only because I found the first few questions impossible!

[5] Khan, presumably

[6] No pressure.

[7] There I go again with the 'no guarantees' thing. Honestly, why can't brains work like the manual says they should?

[8] Except, possibly, a negatively-marked paper, but these are extremely rare.

[9] Or website, I suppose it must be these days, I don't know, when I were a lad we used to get t'exam results on t'stone tablet carried by t'carrier pigeon, if we were lucky!

Printed in Great Britain
by Amazon